Debating

Challenge!

Developing
Major
Debate Skills

Neill Porteous

2

Table of **Contents**

Features

The Debating Challenge series help English learners to develop key debating skills.

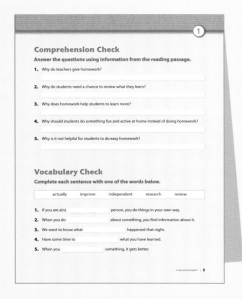

Introduction and Warm-Up Questions

- A variety of activities that introduce each unit's theme to students

- Warm-up questions that allow students to understand major aspects of each unit's theme

Reading

- Carefully chosen debating issues that are relevant to today's teenagers

- Expertly written texts that present different opinions clearly and logically

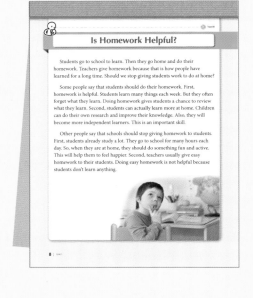

Comprehension Check & Vocabulary Check

- Comprehension questions that help students understand each unit's text

- Vocabulary questions that enable students to learn how to use key words in context

Opinion Practice

- Two different activities that teach learners how to support and refute different opinions

- Various opinions that address major aspects of each unit's debating issue

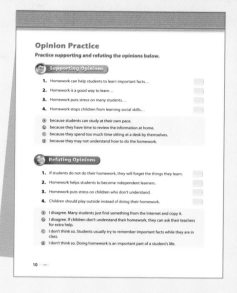

Opinion Examples

- Two different opinions that are based on logical reasoning

- Text analysis activities that reinforce critical reading and thinking skills

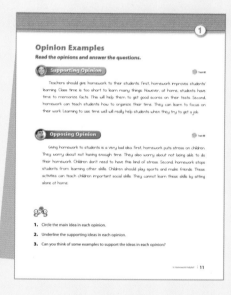

Discussion Questions & Let's Debate

- Discussion questions that are closely associated with each unit's debating issue

- Let's Debate section that invites students to explore and debate major issues

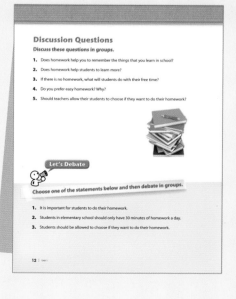

Unit 1
Is Homework Helpful?

Will students study more if their teacher gives them homework? Is homework really helpful? What do you think?

Imagine that you have two hours to finish all the homework below. Decide if the homework is difficult. Then decide how long you will spend on each piece of work.

Homework	Easy or Difficult?	Why?	How Long Will This Homework Take?
Write an essay about a Korean king			
Memorize 30 words for an English test			
Draw a picture of someone in your family			
Find ten facts about a country in Europe			

Total = 2 Hours

Warm-Up Questions

1. What do you think about homework?

2. What do your parents think about homework?

3. What is the strangest homework you have done?

Is Homework Helpful?

Students go to school to learn. Then they go home and do their homework. Teachers give homework because that is how people have learned for a long time. Should we stop giving students work to do at home?

Some people say that students should do their homework. First, homework is helpful. Students learn many things each week. But they often forget what they learn. Doing homework gives students a chance to review what they learn. Second, students can actually learn more at home. Children can do their own research and improve their knowledge. Also, they will become more independent learners. This is an important skill.

Other people say that schools should stop giving homework to students. First, students already study a lot. They go to school for many hours each day. So, when they are at home, they should do something fun and active. This will help them to feel happier. Second, teachers usually give easy homework to their students. Doing easy homework is not helpful because students don't learn anything.

Comprehension Check

Answer the questions using information from the reading passage.

1. Why do teachers give homework?

2. Why do students need a chance to review what they learn?

3. Why does homework help students to learn more?

4. Why should students do something fun and active at home instead of doing homework?

5. Why is it not helpful for students to do easy homework?

Vocabulary Check

Complete each sentence with one of the words below.

actually	improve	independent	research	review

1. If you are a(n) _____ person, you do things in your own way.

2. When you do _____ about something, you find information about it.

3. We want to know what _____ happened that night.

4. Have some time to _____ what you have learned.

5. When you _____ something, it gets better.

Opinion Practice

Practice supporting and refuting the opinions below.

 Supporting Opinions

1. Homework can help students to learn important facts…

2. Homework is a good way to learn…

3. Homework puts stress on many students…

4. Homework stops children from learning social skills…

ⓐ because students can study at their own pace.

ⓑ because they have time to review the information at home.

ⓒ because they spend too much time sitting at a desk by themselves.

ⓓ because they may not understand how to do the homework.

 Refuting Opinions

1. If students do not do their homework, they will forget the things they learn.

2. Homework helps students to become independent learners.

3. Homework puts stress on children who don't understand.

4. Children should play outside instead of doing their homework.

ⓐ I disagree. Many students just find something from the Internet and copy it.

ⓑ I disagree. If children don't understand their homework, they can ask their teachers for extra help.

ⓒ I don't think so. Students usually try to remember important facts while they are in class.

ⓓ I don't think so. Doing homework is an important part of a student's life.

Opinion Examples

Read the opinions and answer the questions.

 Supporting Opinion

 **02** / Unit 1

Teachers should give homework to their students. First, homework improves students' learning. Class time is too short to learn many things. However, at home, students have time to memorize facts. This will help them to get good scores on their tests. Second, homework can teach students how to organize their time. They can learn to focus on their work. Learning to use time well will really help students when they try to get a job.

 Opposing Opinion

 03 / Unit 1

Giving homework to students is a very bad idea. First, homework puts stress on children. They worry about not having enough time. They also worry about not being able to do their homework. Children don't need to have this kind of stress. Second, homework stops students from learning other skills. Children should play sports and make friends. These activities can teach children important social skills. They cannot learn these skills by sitting alone at home.

1. Circle the main idea in each opinion.

2. Underline the supporting ideas in each opinion.

3. Can you think of some examples to support the ideas in each opinion?

Discussion Questions

Discuss these questions in groups.

1. Does homework help you to remember the things that you learn in school?

2. Does homework help students to learn more?

3. If there is no homework, what will students do with their free time?

4. Do you prefer easy homework? Why?

5. Should teachers allow their students to choose if they want to do their homework?

Let's Debate

Choose one of the statements below and then debate in groups.

1. It is important for students to do their homework.

2. Students in elementary school should only have 30 minutes of homework a day.

3. Students should be allowed to choose if they want to do their homework.

Unit 2
Internet Shopping Is the Future

Going shopping can be enjoyable when we buy something exciting such as a new cellphone. Traditionally we have visited department stores or supermarkets. But in the future, we will do all our shopping using the Internet.

Which things do you like to go shopping for? Which things do you dislike buying at stores? Make a list in the table below.

Things I Like Going Shopping for	Things I Dislike Going Shopping for

Warm-Up Questions

1. Do you like to buy things using the Internet?

2. What time of day is best to go shopping? Why?

3. Is it easy to travel to department stores?

Internet Shopping Is the Future

In the past, we went to stores to buy things we needed. These days, however, we can either go shopping or use the Internet. More and more people are choosing to use the Internet to buy things. Is this better than going shopping?

Some people say that it is better to use the Internet to buy products. First, it is much more convenient. Customers can buy any product that they want twenty-four hours a day. Second, people can save time. This is because they don't have to prepare to go out and travel. They don't need to walk around the stores. They can just use their computers or smartphones to buy the products that they want.

Other people say that going shopping is better than using the Internet. First, when people go shopping, they can touch and try the products. As a result, they will be happy with the things they buy. Second, going shopping is a lot of fun. Families and friends can meet and look around the stores. They can also eat nice food or stop at a café. This is much better than sitting at home all day.

Comprehension Check

Answer the questions using information from the reading passage.

1. Where did we go in the past to buy things we needed?

2. Why can shopping using the Internet be more convenient?

3. How can people save time by shopping on the Internet?

4. Why will people be happy buying products in stores?

5. What makes going to the stores more fun than Internet shopping?

Vocabulary Check

Complete each sentence with one of the words below.

café	customer	preparing	product	try

1. A _____ is something that is made so that people can use it.

2. You'd better _____ on the dress before you buy it.

3. We spent a lot of time _____ to go on vacation.

4. A _____ is a person who buys things from a store.

5. A _____ is a small restaurant where you can eat simple meals.

Opinion Practice

Practice supporting and refuting the opinions below.

 Supporting Opinions

1. People spend less money when they use the Internet to buy things…

2. There is more choice on the Internet…

3. It is much faster to buy things at the stores…

4. Going shopping can be fun…

ⓐ because the customer can take the item home quickly.

ⓑ because it is much cheaper.

ⓒ because they give free samples to eat and drink.

ⓓ because you can use websites from different countries.

 Refuting Opinions

1. Shopping on the Internet is much faster.

2. It is fun to go shopping.

3. Customers can get great deals by shopping on the Internet.

4. Going shopping can be a healthy activity.

ⓐ I don't think so. People eat junk foods and don't move very much.

ⓑ I don't think so. Many Internet companies sell bad products, and these products can be dangerous.

ⓒ I disagree. People need to type a lot of information and then wait for the package to arrive.

ⓓ I disagree. It puts stress on us. We get stuck in traffic jams and the stores are often too crowded.

Opinion Examples

Read the opinions and answer the questions.

 Supporting Opinion

The best way to buy products is by using the Internet. First, websites are usually much cheaper than stores. In addition, they often give a free gift. On the other hand, stores are expensive. We usually need to pay money to travel to the stores. Second, the Internet gives us more choice. Shoppers can look at many different websites in Korea and other countries. As a result, Internet shoppers can choose from thousands of different products.

 Opposing Opinion

Shopping on the Internet may be fun. But going to real stores is much better. First, it is much faster than shopping on the Internet. If we need to buy something, we can buy it right away at a store. If we buy it on the Internet, we need to wait more than a day. Second, if we go to shopping malls or department stores, we know that we are buying real products. We are not buying false products. When we shop on the Internet, we don't know if we are buying real products.

1. Circle the main idea in each opinion.

2. Underline the supporting ideas in each opinion.

3. Can you think of some examples to support the ideas in each opinion?

Discussion Questions

Discuss these questions in groups.

1. Do you prefer shopping on the Internet?

2. Is it a good thing to be able to buy things twenty-four hours a day?

3. Do you think it is faster to buy things on the Internet?

4. Do you like to try a product before you buy it? Why?

5. Is it less stressful to shop online than to shop in a store?

Let's Debate

Choose one of the statements below and then debate in groups.

1. It is better to shop on the Internet than to go to the store.

2. Shopping malls and department stores will never disappear.

3. It is healthier for people to go shopping than to use the Internet to buy things.

Unit 3
All Students Should Have Work Experience

Many students don't know much about the job they choose. They don't know what jobs they want to do, either. Having work experience can solve these problems.

Imagine you are going to have work experience. Think where you want to work. Plan your schedule using the table below.

Where I Want to Work:	
Start Time: _____ Lunchtime: _____ to _____ Finish Time: _____	
Morning	
Lunchtime	
Afternoon	

Warm-Up Questions

1. Do you want to have work experience instead of going to school?

2. How long should work experience be?

3. Will you choose a job you like? Or do you prefer an easy job?

All Students Should Have Work Experience

In many countries, middle school students have work experience for one or two weeks. They work at companies or other businesses. This experience can be very helpful. Should all Korean middle school students have work experience too?

Some people say that students should have work experience. First, they can find out what it is like to work in a real job. If workers don't do their jobs well, they will get in a lot of trouble. They may be fired. Students need to learn about this. Second, students can try a job that they want to have. After they experience the job, they can decide whether they really want to have that job. If they don't like the job, they can think about getting a different job.

Other people say that work experience is not useful for middle school students. First, work experience is too short. They cannot learn much in one or two weeks. Therefore, it is better for them to stay in school and study. Second, companies don't let students do important work. This is because the students may make errors. As a result, students on work experience usually waste their time doing simple jobs. They may make coffee or photocopy documents.

Comprehension Check

Answer the questions using information from the reading passage.

1. How long does most work experience last?

2. What happens if workers don't do their jobs well?

3. What can students do if they don't like a particular job?

4. Why is it better for students to stay in school and study?

5. Why do students on work experience usually waste their time?

Vocabulary Check

Complete each sentence with one of the words below.

businesses	document	fires	let	photocopy

1. When you _____ something, you make a paper copy of it.

2. Her father does not _____ her date a young boy.

3. The actor read the _____ carefully before he signed it.

4. Stores and factories are examples of _____.

5. If your company _____ you, you lose your job.

Opinion Practice

Practice supporting and refuting the opinions below.

 Supporting Opinions

1. Middle school students should not work with adults…

2. Students shouldn't waste their time having work experience…

3. It is important for students to have work experience…

4. Work experience can help students to get jobs…

ⓐ because they can see what it is like to work in a company.

ⓑ because they will not learn any important skills.

ⓒ because companies may ask the students to work for them when they are older.

ⓓ because they are still children.

 Refuting Opinions

1. Students don't learn anything important during work experience.

2. Students usually have to do jobs that they are not interested in.

3. Work experience is really enjoyable.

4. During work experience, students can learn more about their favorite jobs.

ⓐ I disagree. During work experience, students cannot do important things, so they cannot learn much about their favorite jobs.

ⓑ I disagree. Students learn what it is like to work in the real world.

ⓒ I don't think so. Students often get tired because they need to work many hours.

ⓓ I don't think so. Companies usually allow students to choose jobs.

Opinion Examples

Read the opinions and answer the questions.

 Supporting Opinion

 08 / Unit 3

Korean middle school students should have work experience. First, students can learn more about working in companies. They can learn about particular jobs. They can also learn important skills such as how to organize their work. Second, work experience can help students to get jobs when they are older. This is because a company always needs workers. If they like a student's work, the business can offer a job to that student.

 Opposing Opinion

 **09** / Unit 3

Korean middle school students do not need work experience. First, middle school students are young teenagers. They are too young to work with adults at a real company. Students are still learning and make many errors. Students will be worried about making mistakes during their work experience. Second, students don't learn any new or important skills. Companies will not spend a lot of time and money training students. This is because the students will go back to school in one or two weeks.

1. Circle the main idea in each opinion.

2. Underline the supporting ideas in each opinion.

3. Can you think of some examples to support the ideas in each opinion?

Discussion Questions

Discuss these questions in groups.

1. What can students do if they don't like their work experience?

2. Do you think you can learn more by having work experience?

3. Should students work the same hours as adults during their work experience?

4. Do you worry about making mistakes during work experience?

5. At what age should students have work experience?

Let's Debate

Choose one of the statements below and then debate in groups.

1. All middle school students should have work experience.

2. Students should have work experience twice a year.

3. Teachers should allow their students to choose whether they want to have work experience.

Unit 4
Internet Cafés: Good Fun or Dangerous?

Korean children go to Internet cafés to play online computer games. Internet cafés are very popular. But are they good places for children to spend their time?

Imagine that you have some free time. You decide to go to an Internet café to play your favorite online computer game. You have ₩5,000 in your pocket. How do you want to spend your money?

One-Hour Play	Soft Drink	Chocolate	Instant Noodles (Ramen)	Kimbap
₩1,000	₩500	₩500	₩1,000	₩1,500

Explain how you want to spend your money. Why do you want to spend it this way? (Remember you cannot spend more than ₩5,000.)

Warm-Up Questions

1. Have you ever been to an Internet café? What did you think?

2. What do your parents think about Internet cafés?

3. Is it better to play computer games in an Internet café or at home? Why?

Internet Cafés: Good Fun or Dangerous?

Korean children love to play computer games. There are thousands of Internet cafés across Korea. Many children go to these Internet cafés to have fun. But are they putting themselves in danger by spending time in these places?

Some people say that going to Internet cafés is just good fun. First, Internet cafés are very cheap. Children can spend several hours playing their favorite games for very little money. If they want to do other activities, such as skiing, they need to spend a lot of money. Second, Internet cafés are great places to meet friends and play together. In Korea, it is often too hot or too cold to be outside. However, Internet cafés are always at the perfect temperature. So, they are very comfortable places.

Other people say that Internet cafés are dangerous. First, children can use the Internet freely. This is a problem because the Internet contains many bad things. These things are not helpful to children. Some of them may put the children in danger. Second, children spend too much time playing computer games. This is a serious problem because the children cannot do other healthy activities.

Comprehension Check

Answer the questions using information from the reading passage.

1. Are there many Internet cafés in Korea?

2. Why can children spend several hours in Internet cafés for very little money?

3. Why are Internet cafés great places to meet friends?

4. Why is it a problem if children can use the Internet freely in Internet cafés?

5. What can happen if children spend too much time playing computer games?

Vocabulary Check

Complete each sentence with one of the words below.

contains	dangerous	freely	perfect	temperature

1. If you can do something _____, nobody stops you from doing it.

2. The _____ of something shows how hot or cold it is.

3. Scientists say that milk _____ bad things.

4. Luckily, the weather was _____.

5. If something is _____, it can hurt or harm you.

Opinion Practice

Practice supporting and refuting the opinions below.

 Supporting Opinions

1. Internet cafés are not healthy places for children…

2. Internet cafés are good places to make new friends…

3. Playing computer games in an Internet café is really great…

4. Children can spend too much money in Internet cafés…

ⓐ because the chairs are comfortable and the Internet is very fast.

ⓑ because they are too dark and some people smoke.

ⓒ because they buy a lot of snacks and soft drinks.

ⓓ because children can meet people who have the same hobby.

 Refuting Opinions

1. Children spend too much money in Internet cafés.

2. Internet cafés are safe places for children to meet their friends.

3. Young people who go to Internet cafés do not do other healthy activities.

4. Korean children are too busy to spend many hours playing games in an Internet café.

ⓐ I don't think so. Because they are busy, Korean children need to have some fun in Internet cafés.

ⓑ I don't think so. Children don't have to spend much money. They can just pay to use the computer.

ⓒ I disagree. Internet cafés are not safe. Children can meet bad people in the Internet café and online.

ⓓ I disagree. Young people who go to Internet cafés do other outdoor activities.

Opinion Examples

Read the opinions and answer the questions.

 Supporting Opinion

 **11** / Unit 4

Internet cafés are great places for children to have fun. First, Internet cafés are very comfortable. Customers can sit in soft chairs and use new computers. Because of this, Internet cafés are excellent places to spend free time. Second, children can make new friends when they visit Internet cafés. It is easy to become friends when you meet someone who has the same hobby as you. Making good friends is very positive.

 Opposing Opinion

 **12** / Unit 4

Children should not go to Internet cafés to play computer games. First, the Internet café is unhealthy. It is very dark. This is bad for children's eyesight. Also, many adults continue to smoke in Internet cafés. They do not care about the health of young children. Second, children spend too much money while playing games. They pay to use the computer and to buy snacks and soft drinks. After playing for a few hours, children will have spent too much money.

1. Circle the main idea in each opinion.

2. Underline the supporting ideas in each opinion.

3. Can you think of some examples to support the ideas in each opinion?

Discussion Questions

Discuss these questions in groups.

1. Do you think that Internet cafés are safe for children?

2. Are Internet cafés good places to meet your friends?

3. Do you think Internet cafés are cheap?

4. Is it safe for children to use the Internet by themselves?

5. At what age should a child be allowed to go to an Internet café without an adult?

Let's Debate

Choose one of the statements below and then debate in groups.

1. Internet cafés are good places for children to go to.

2. Internet cafés should be more expensive so that children can only play for a short time.

3. Parents should stop their children from using Internet cafés.

Unit 5
One Global Language

There are more than 6,000 languages in the world. This is a problem because people from different countries cannot understand each other. Will one global language be better for everyone?

Some English words may seem quite strange. Look at the list of words below and try to think of a new name that is simpler. An example has been done for you.

Pencil	writing stick
Hamburger	
Window	
Television	
Restaurant	
Swimming	

Warm-Up Questions

1. Should each country have its own language?

2. Do you like to learn foreign languages?

3. How many languages do we need to learn?

One Global Language

Different countries have different languages. As a result, it is hard to understand people from different nations. If we use only one language, will the world be a better place to live?

Some people say that all countries should use one language. First, we can easily communicate with anybody. As a result, we can learn about other people's lives. When we understand each other well, we can help each other. This may stop us from fighting wars. Second, we can travel anywhere in the world and feel comfortable. We sometimes feel scared when we travel to a country that speaks a different language. Such things will not happen if all countries use one common language.

Other people say that we should not have a common language. First, the native speakers of a common language will have an advantage. If we choose Chinese as our common language, the Chinese people will be more successful than others. Second, most of the world's languages will die out. This is already happening because many people want to learn English. Losing even more languages will be terrible.

Comprehension Check

Answer the questions using information from the reading passage.

1. Why is it hard to understand people from different nations?

2. If we speak a common language, we may stop fighting each other. Why?

3. How do people feel when they travel to a country that speaks a different language?

4. Why is it not fair to use one global language?

5. What will happen to many languages if we use one global language?

Vocabulary Check

Complete each sentence with one of the words below.

advantage	common	global	nations	scared

1. Many young children are _____ of spiders.

2. There are about 200 _____ in the world.

3. If two countries have a(n) _____ language, they share the language.

4. If you have a(n) _____, it helps you to become better than others.

5. A(n) _____ problem is a problem that the whole world needs to solve.

Opinion Practice

Practice supporting and refuting the opinions below.

 Supporting Opinions

1. The world will be richer if there is one common language…

2. Most people will feel unhappy with one global language…

3. We do not need to have one common language…

4. A global language helps us to have friends from all around the world…

ⓐ because we can easily speak to each other using the global language.

ⓑ because many languages will die out.

ⓒ because most people don't communicate with people from other countries.

ⓓ because companies can sell more things around the world.

 Refuting Opinions

1. People can communicate easily if we speak one language.

2. The world will be a happier place if we speak one language.

3. Native speakers of a global language can get better jobs than people who need to learn the language.

4. Too many languages will die out if we only use one global language.

ⓐ I disagree. People will be unhappy about losing their languages.

ⓑ I disagree. It will take a long time for everyone to learn the global language.

ⓒ I don't think that is a problem. It is only natural for languages to die out.

ⓓ I don't think that is a problem. There are always many jobs for people.

Opinion Examples

Read the opinions and answer the questions.

 Supporting Opinion

 **14** / Unit 5

The world needs to have one common language. First, all the people in the world can communicate with each other. That will be great because we can learn about each other's lives and cultures. Second, the world will be richer. This is because companies from all over the world can work together. At the moment, many companies cannot trade because they are unable to communicate well. More trade will mean more jobs for everyone.

 Opposing Opinion

 15 / Unit 5

I strongly disagree with the idea of a global language. First, most people do not want a global language. They will be very unhappy if they cannot use their own language. In fact, the idea of a global language will fail. This is because people will continue to use their own native languages. Second, we don't need a global language. Only a few people communicate with individuals and companies from other countries. Most people only need their own language to be successful.

1. Circle the main idea in each opinion.

2. Underline the supporting ideas in each opinion.

3. Can you think of some examples to support the ideas in each opinion?

Discussion Questions

Discuss these questions in groups.

1. Will you stop speaking Korean and use another language if you can be more successful?

2. Will people communicate easily if we speak one common language?

3. Will trips to different countries be better if there is a global language?

4. Which language should we choose as the global language?

5. Is it a problem if more languages die out?

Choose one of the statements below and then debate in groups.

1. We should have one global language.

2. English should be the global language.

3. We should create a new language for a global language.

Unit 6
Computer-Graded Essays

Students write a lot of essays during their time at school. Essays take a long time to write, and teachers need to grade them. Some schools are now using computers to grade essays. Is this a good idea?

Computers can do so many things. Do you prefer a computer or human to do the jobs listed below?

Job	Computer or Human	Reasons
Driver		
Doctor		
Judge		
Teacher		

Warm-Up Questions

1. Do you like writing essays?

2. Do you think teachers like grading essays?

3. Does writing essays help students learn better?

Computer-Graded Essays

Students write essays to show their understanding of a subject. Some essays are very long. And they take a long time to write. Then, teachers need to spend many hours grading the essays. Will computer-graded essays help everyone?

Some people say that using computers to grade essays is much better. First, computers can grade essays very quickly. In fact, computers can grade thousands of essays in a few seconds. As a result, students will get their grades and feedback right away. Second, students can write more essays. At the moment, teachers only give a few essays to students. This is because they don't have time to grade lots of writing. If teachers use computers to grade essays, students will benefit by doing more writing.

Other people say that we should not use computers to grade essays. First, computers cannot grade as well as humans. Computers cannot decide if the students' ideas are strong or weak. As a result, computers often give essays the wrong score. Second, students can learn how to get a high score. All they need to do is write very long sentences and paragraphs. They also need to use difficult words. But this is not why we write essays.

Comprehension Check

Answer the questions using information from the reading passage.

1. Why do students write essays?

2. How fast can computers grade essays?

3. Why don't teachers give students many essays at the moment?

4. Why can computers not grade essays as well as humans?

5. How can students get a high score on computer-graded essays?

Vocabulary Check

Complete each sentence with one of the words below.

benefit	feedback	grade	human	seconds

1. The word _____ means "a person."

2. There are sixty _____ in a minute.

3. You can _____ a lot from reading books.

4. Her _____ helped us to improve our work.

5. If you _____ something, you say how good it is.

Opinion Practice

Practice supporting and refuting the opinions below.

 Supporting Opinions

1. Students can improve faster when computers grade their essays…

2. Using computers to grade essays is not a good idea…

3. Teaching will improve if essays are computer-graded…

4. Teachers don't always give the correct score…

ⓐ because teachers will have much more time to plan their classes.

ⓑ because the computers don't know if the facts are correct.

ⓒ because they sometimes give higher scores to students they like.

ⓓ because they will get feedback right away.

 Refuting Opinions

1. Computer-graded essays will be just as accurate as essays graded by teachers.

2. Students can benefit from getting quick feedback.

3. Students who always type their essays will not have good handwriting.

4. Computer-graded essays will make students learn to use difficult words.

ⓐ I don't think so. Computers do not just look at the difficulty of the vocabulary. They look at how the student organizes his or her essay.

ⓑ I don't think so. Computers only look at the number of words and the difficulty of the vocabulary.

ⓒ I disagree. Students just look at the score and ignore the other information.

ⓓ I disagree. Students can learn to write well and still type their essays.

Opinion Examples

Read the opinions and answer the questions.

 Supporting Opinion

 **17** / Unit 6

Using computers to grade essays is an excellent idea. First, teaching will improve. At the moment, teachers spend many hours grading essays and giving feedback. If they don't need to do that, they can spend more time preparing for classes. Then, their classes will become more interesting. Second, students will get quick feedback. As a result, they can rewrite their essays and submit them again. Students will get higher grades and learn more.

 Opposing Opinion

 **18** / Unit 6

Computer-graded essays are a bad idea. First, computers only look at the number of words and the vocabulary the students use. The most important thing in an essay is that students show their understanding. We don't always need to use long sentences and difficult words. Second, computers don't know if the students' information is correct. If a student writes an essay with excellent grammar but all the facts are wrong, he or she will still get a very high score. This does not help anyone.

1. Circle the main idea in each opinion.

2. Underline the supporting ideas in each opinion.

3. Can you think of some examples to support the ideas in each opinion?

Discussion Questions

Discuss these questions in groups.

1. Do you want a computer to grade your essays?

2. Is it important for students to get quick feedback about their essays?

3. Do you want to write more essays?

4. Do you want your teachers to spend more time planning your lessons?

5. Do you read the teacher's feedback and follow the advice?

Choose one of the statements below and then debate in groups.

1. Computer-graded essays are an excellent idea.

2. Great ideas are more important than grammar.

3. Essays are much better than multiple choice tests.

Unit 7
Children's Privacy

These days, the world is becoming more dangerous. As a result, parents are always checking what their children are doing. Therefore, many children have no privacy. Is this acceptable?

Read the problems below and decide if you think the parents are doing the right thing. Then explain your reasons.

David was unhappy because his parents blocked all the television channels except the educational and news channels. They did this because David watched TV for many hours a day without doing his homework.

Emma's parents always check how much money she has in her room. They do this because Emma once stole some cash from her uncle. Emma thinks this needs to stop because she knows she did a bad thing. She is also sorry that she did it.

Warm-Up Questions

1. Should parents always check where their children are?

2. At what age should children have more freedom?

3. Are there any places that children should not go on their own?

Children's Privacy

All people, including children, have secrets that they want to keep private. But children often have no privacy. This is because their parents always want to know everything that they are doing. Are the parents doing the right thing?

Some people say that it is important for children to have privacy. Parents think they are protecting their children by knowing all their secrets. But they are wrong. Children learn by making mistakes. Therefore, parents should give their children more freedom to learn from their errors. Another problem is that children with no privacy feel very unhappy. Nobody likes to be watched all the time. As a result, overprotective parents and their children usually have bad relationships.

Other people say that children's privacy is a bad thing. Too many things, such as cellphones and the Internet, can cause children to get into trouble. Therefore, parents need to check their children's phones and computers all the time. In addition, parents should be able to check what their children are doing. This is because they are responsible for their children. Parents need to know that their children are doing their homework, sleeping well, and not getting into trouble.

Comprehension Check

Answer the questions using information from the reading passage.

1. Why do children often have no privacy?

2. Why is it important for children to make mistakes?

3. What kind of relationship do overprotective parents and their children have?

4. Why can it be a problem if children use cellphones and the Internet?

5. What is the reason why parents should be able to check on their children all the time?

Vocabulary Check

Complete each sentence with one of the words below.

freedom	including	overprotective	private	protect

1. If you _____ your daughter, you keep her safe from danger.

2. _____ information is information that is secret or personal.

3. Many students, _____ Ashley, objected to the plan.

4. In the past, slaves had no _____ .

5. _____ parents do not allow their children to do many things.

Opinion Practice

Practice supporting and refuting the opinions below.

 Supporting Opinions

1. Parents need to know what their children are doing…

2. Children need freedom to make mistakes…

3. It is fine for parents to check their children's phones and computers…

4. It is important for children to have privacy…

ⓐ because that is how we learn important lessons.

ⓑ because they are too young to protect themselves.

ⓒ because they pay for everything.

ⓓ because they will be unhappy if they cannot keep anything secret.

 Refuting Opinions

1. Children should be allowed to use their phones and computers in private.

2. Parents always check on their children because they love them.

3. Parents should be able to know where their children are all the time.

4. It is important to give children privacy even if they do something silly.

ⓐ I disagree. When children do something very bad, they can get into a lot of trouble.

ⓑ I disagree. Parents should trust their children to look after themselves.

ⓒ I don't think so. Parents need to protect their children from dangerous people who use the Internet.

ⓓ I don't think so. Many parents don't think about how their children feel. They don't love them.

Opinion Examples

Read the opinions and answer the questions.

 Supporting Opinion

 **20** / Unit 7

I believe that all children should have privacy. One reason is that young people need to have freedom to make mistakes. We can learn a lot by doing something wrong. Our parents cannot protect us forever. We need to learn to take care of ourselves. Another reason is that children with no privacy are unhappy. Everybody has secrets that they do not want to share. If parents keep trying to find out what their children are doing, the relationship between the children and their parents will be terrible.

 Opposing Opinion

 **21** / Unit 7

Children should not have privacy. To begin with, parents need to protect their children from bad people, such as bullies. Parents need to know everything about their children if they want to keep them safe. They need to check their children's messages and emails to protect their children. In addition, parents should make sure that their children are not doing anything bad. We learn from our mistakes, but sometimes children do some very bad things. This is because they do not always understand what they are doing.

1. Circle the main idea in each opinion.

2. Underline the supporting ideas in each opinion.

3. Can you think of some examples to support the ideas in each opinion?

Discussion Questions

Discuss these questions in groups.

1. Are you happy to let your parents check your text messages and emails?

2. How will you feel if your parents always want to know where you are?

3. Should children be allowed to lock their bedroom doors so that they can have privacy?

4. Should parents give their children total freedom?

5. Should parents let their children make mistakes if it helps them to learn?

Let's Debate

Choose one of the statements below and then debate in groups.

1. It is important for children to have privacy.

2. Parents who pay for their children's cellphones should be allowed to check their phones.

3. Children's bedrooms should be private.

Unit 8
Asking for Advice

Young people have a lot of things to learn about the world. When they need advice about something, is it better to ask their parents or to ask their friends?

The following people need advice. Read their problems and decide what they should do. Discuss your ideas with your classmates.

Problem	Advice
I am supposed to go on a family vacation. But my best friend wants me to go on vacation with her family. I don't know what to do.	
I broke the window at the entrance of our apartment building. Should I say I did it? Or should I just keep quiet?	
I cheated on a school test. I'm not sure if my teacher knows. Should I tell him what I did?	

Warm-Up Questions

1. What are some things that people need advice about?

2. Is it easy or difficult to ask someone for advice?

3. Do you listen to the advice people give you?

DC2-08
MP3

Asking for Advice

As children and teenagers get older, they need to think about education, jobs, and relationships. They have choices to make. So, they need advice. Should they ask their parents or should they ask their friends?

Some people say that young people should always ask their parents for advice. One reason is that parents are older and have more experience. Parents are more likely to know the solution to their children's problems. This is because they had similar questions when they were younger. Another reason is that parents will give the most truthful advice. This is because they love and care for their children. Parents really don't want to see their children upset.

Other people say that young people should ask their friends for advice. Young people spend a lot of time together at school and in their free time. As a result, they know each other really well. Therefore, they can give the most suitable advice. Another reason is that friends will be a similar age and understand things much better than parents. Parents don't understand their teenage children because the world has changed a lot since they were young.

Comprehension Check

Answer the questions using information from the reading passage.

1. What are some of the things young people think about as they get older?

2. Why is it an advantage that parents are older and more experienced?

3. Why will parents always give truthful advice?

4. Why do young people know each other really well?

5. Why don't parents usually understand their teenage children?

Vocabulary Check

Complete each sentence with one of the words below.

suitable	solution	upset	truthful	similar

1. My best friend and I are very _____. We like exactly the same things.

2. I like math class because there is always a correct _____.

3. It is important to always be _____. We shouldn't lie.

4. I was _____ when I lost my bag on vacation.

5. Basketball is a(n) _____ hobby for me because I am very tall.

Opinion Practice

Practice supporting and refuting the opinions below.

 Supporting Opinions

1. Friends may not give the best advice…

2. It is difficult to talk to parents about some things…

3. Asking parents for advice can cause arguments…

4. It is easy for young people to ask their friends for advice…

ⓐ because they spend a lot of time together each day.

ⓑ because they are jealous of people who may become more successful than them.

ⓒ because they may strongly disagree.

ⓓ because parents always think that their advice is correct.

 Refuting Opinions

1. Friends understand each other much better than parents do.

2. It is much easier for young people to ask friends for advice because they are always together.

3. Friends always give the best advice.

4. It is better to ask parents for advice because they understand their children's situation.

ⓐ I disagree. Young people don't care about each other.

ⓑ I disagree. Parents have taken care of their children since they were born. They know much more about their children.

ⓒ I'm not sure about this. Most teenagers spend very little time with their parents and don't tell them much about their lives.

ⓓ No, they don't. People give advice that their friends want to hear.

Opinion Examples

Read the opinions and answer the questions.

 Supporting Opinion

 **23** / Unit 8

The best people to ask for advice are parents. One reason is that parents will always give the best advice for their children. Parents love their children, so they will give them advice that is honest and truthful. Friends don't always do this because they worry it may end their friendship. Another reason is that parents understand their children's thinking and personality. This is because they have taken care of them since they were born. It is a bad idea to ask advice from a friend you have known for a short time.

 Opposing Opinion

 **24** / Unit 8

If a young person needs advice, the smartest thing to do is to ask his or her friends. Good friends can talk about any problem and find a solution together. That is not possible with parents. This is because they always think that their advice is correct. The parents may get angry talking about some topics. In addition, young people spend a lot of time together. As a result, they understand how their friend is feeling at that moment. Parents cannot understand their children so well because they are too busy doing other things.

1. Circle the main idea in each opinion.

2. Underline the supporting ideas in each opinion.

3. Can you think of some examples to support the ideas in each opinion?

Discussion Questions

Discuss these questions in groups.

1. Do you think your parents know you better than your friends?

2. What things are difficult to talk to your parents about? Why?

3. Will you give a friend truthful advice even if it upsets him or her?

4. Will you contact your parents if you need quick advice?

5. Do you think your friends will ask you for honest advice?

Let's Debate

Choose one of the statements below and then debate in groups.

1. It is better for young people to ask their parents for advice.

2. Parents give more truthful advice than friends.

3. People should only give advice about things they fully understand.

Unit 9
Closing Stores on Sundays

These days, almost all stores are open on Sundays. This is because they want customers to come and buy products. Will it be better if stores close on Sundays?

Imagine that no stores are open on a Sunday. There are some things that you really need today, but you cannot buy them. Think of ways to get the items you need. (Only use an answer one time)

Item	How You Will Get It or Make It
Fruit Juice	
Soap	
Dinner	
Toothbrush	

Warm-Up Questions

1. Do you like to go shopping on Sundays?

2. What do you think is the best day to go shopping?

3. How will you feel if no stores are open on Sundays?

Closing Stores on Sundays

We can go shopping seven days a week, and some stores are even open twenty-four hours a day. This may be very convenient. But closing stores on Sundays may improve our society.

Some people say that there are many benefits of closing stores on Sundays. One advantage is that families will spend more time together. If families don't go shopping, they can do fun activities. They can go to the park or just talk to each other. Another advantage is that families can save money. When people go shopping, they usually purchase things that they don't need. Therefore, if stores are closed on Sundays, families will not waste their money.

Other people say that it is not a good idea to close stores on Sundays. One problem is that most people only have time to go shopping on Sundays. This is because they work from Monday through Friday. Some people even work on Saturdays, too. Another disadvantage is that many individuals will lose their part-time jobs. For example, high school and university students often work on Sundays to earn money. They cannot work during the week because they need to study.

Comprehension Check

Answer the questions using information from the reading passage.

1. How often can we go shopping?

2. What kinds of things can families do together if stores are closed on Sundays?

3. Why will people not waste their money if stores are not open on Sundays?

4. Why do most people need to go shopping on Sundays?

5. Who may lose their jobs if stores do not open on Sundays? Why?

Vocabulary Check

Complete each sentence with one of the words below.

disadvantage	earn	individual	purchase	society

1. I want a job where I can _____ a lot of money.

2. Only one _____ can walk across the bridge at a time.

3. You don't have to _____ this expensive smartphone.

4. Its _____ is that we cannot use it in cold weather.

5. There are many ways to improve our _____ .

Opinion Practice

Practice supporting and refuting the opinions below.

 Supporting Opinions

1. Stores need to close on Sundays…

2. It is better for store workers not to work on Sundays…

3. Stores should be allowed to open whenever they want…

4. We need stores to be open on Sundays…

ⓐ because we can choose if we want to go shopping or not.

ⓑ because we need to stop buying things we don't need.

ⓒ because the workers can spend time with their families at home.

ⓓ because sometimes we need to buy things right away.

 Refuting Opinions

1. If stores close on Sundays, store workers will earn less money.

2. Families will spend more time together if stores close on Sundays.

3. We need stores to open on Sundays so that we can buy the things we need.

4. Korea's economy will become bad if stores close on Sundays.

ⓐ This is unlikely. People will still go shopping to buy things. They just won't do that on Sundays.

ⓑ This is not true. Stores are open many hours each day. Workers do not need to work less.

ⓒ Not really. We just need to write a list of the things we need and buy them on a different day.

ⓓ Families *do* spend time together when they go shopping on Sundays. They often have lunch or dinner together, too. That is quality family time.

Opinion Examples

Read the opinions and answer the questions.

 Supporting Opinion

All stores must be closed on Sundays. To begin with, people will spend less money. These days, people in our society buy things that they don't really need. In fact, some shoppers purchase so many items that they do not have enough money to pay for other important things such as bills. In addition, if stores close on Sundays, the store workers can spend time with their families and friends. We spend too much time working or traveling to our jobs. It is important that we have enough time to relax with people we care about.

 Opposing Opinion

It is not a good idea to close stores on Sundays. The first reason is that in our society, people should be allowed to go shopping whenever they want. If they want to go shopping on Sundays, they should be free to do that. Stores will close on Sundays if there are no customers. The second reason is that shopping on a Sunday is a great time for families to be together. On Sundays, families are usually relaxed. As a result, they can take their time walking around the stores and chatting with each other. They may also sit down and relax by eating ice cream or having drinks. That is great family time.

1. Circle the main idea in each opinion.

2. Underline the supporting ideas in each opinion.

3. Can you think of some examples to support the ideas in each opinion?

Discussion Questions

Discuss these questions in groups.

1. Do you think most families like to go shopping on Sundays?

2. Do you think people will spend less money if stores are closed on Sundays?

3. Is it a problem if students cannot do part-time jobs on Sundays?

4. Is Sunday the best day for stores to close? Explain your reasons.

5. Will families spend more time together on Sundays if all the stores are closed?

Let's Debate

Choose one of the statements below and then debate in groups.

1. All stores should close on Sundays.

2. Only large stores and supermarkets should be closed on Sundays.

3. Stores should only be allowed to open for six hours on a Sunday.

Unit 10
Should School Sports Be Optional?

Does every student need to take part in sports class? Will it be better if students can choose if they want to play sports in school?

Think of your best and worst sports classes at school. Explain why you really liked or disliked the classes. Discuss your ideas with classmates.

Sports Classes I Enjoyed	Reasons

Sports Classes I Disliked	Reasons

Warm-Up Questions

1. Do you like physical education class at school? Why? Why not?

2. How many P.E. classes do you have at school each week? Do you want more sports classes?

3. What is the most important reason to have P.E. classes?

Should School Sports Be Optional?

At school, children have to learn subjects such as Korean, math, science, English, and physical education. Students will always need Korean, and many will need English for jobs. But do we really need physical education class? Should students be allowed to choose if they want to do P.E.?

Some people say that school sports should be optional. Some students are bad at sports and worry so much about P.E. They even don't want to go to school. Students who feel like this should be allowed to study a different subject. Another reason why school sports should be optional is that students feel tired. P.E. class is hard. Some students feel exhausted after sports class. As a result, they cannot concentrate on other lessons at school.

Other people say that every student should do P.E. Sports class is an important lesson. One benefit is that it helps us to be healthy. Many children around the world are becoming obese. This is because they sit down for too long and eat unhealthy snacks. P.E. class can help keep them in shape. Another benefit is that students learn many important skills. They learn about team work and communication. They learn not to quit. These are useful life skills.

Comprehension Check

Answer the questions using information from the reading passage.

1. Why do many students need to learn English?

2. What can happen when students are really worried about P.E. class?

3. Why is it a problem if students are tired after P.E. class?

4. Why are many children becoming obese?

5. What life skills can students learn in sports class?

Vocabulary Check

Complete each sentence with one of the words below.

exhausted	obese	optional	quit	shape

1. If we eat too much junk food, we will become _____.

2. I was _____ after playing and swimming at the beach all day.

3. I had to _____ playing for my soccer team because I moved to a new city.

4. Jogging and cycling helps me to stay in _____.

5. If something is _____, you can decide whether you want to do it or not.

Opinion Practice

Practice supporting and refuting the opinions below.

 Supporting Opinions

1. Physical education class can help students study better…

2. Sports class is not important for our future…

3. Playing sports can be dangerous…

4. Exercise is important for students' health…

ⓐ because we can get badly hurt.

ⓑ because they feel refreshed after exercising and can focus on their work.

ⓒ because it doesn't help us to get good jobs.

ⓓ because they can get in shape.

 Refuting Opinions

1. We don't need to be good at sports to enjoy them.

2. Students are too tired to study after P.E. class.

3. We can try a lot of new sports and find a new hobby.

4. Sports class doesn't help students get good jobs when they are older.

ⓐ This is not true. Students learn many skills that they can use when they get jobs and they can also stay healthy.

ⓑ This is not a problem because they will become fitter and not feel tired after a few sports lessons.

ⓒ People who are not good at sports don't feel like this. They don't like being the worst.

ⓓ Students don't go to school to find a hobby. They go to school to learn.

Opinion Examples

Read the opinions and answer the questions.

 Supporting Opinion

Students should be allowed to choose if they want to have physical education class. One reason is that sports do not help people to get into good universities or get good jobs. Students should use the time to study really important subjects. Another reason is that some students are very bad at playing sports. Even though they try really hard, they feel bad because they make mistakes or always lose. This is very embarrassing for the students. It will be much better if students can study something that they enjoy.

 Opposing Opinion

Every student has to do physical education. To begin with, P.E. class helps students to be healthy and fit. Students who are in shape have less stress and can study for longer. As a result, their school scores can improve. Another great thing about sports class is that we learn many skills that we can use all the time. Sports teach us leadership, communication, and many other things. These are skills that can help people to get good jobs.

1. Circle the main idea in each opinion.

2. Underline the supporting ideas in each opinion.

3. Can you think of some examples to support the ideas in each opinion?

Discussion Questions

Discuss these questions in groups.

1. Is sports class an important lesson?

2. What skills do you think you learn in your P.E. classes?

3. Should students be allowed to choose what sports they play?

4. Is it a problem if some students are really bad at sports?

5. If students don't do P.E. in school, what should they do instead?

Let's Debate

Choose one of the statements below and then debate in groups.

1. School sports should be optional.

2. Students should be allowed to decide whether they want to have sports class.

3. Students who choose not to do sports need to do something active.

Unit 11
Live Alone or with Other People?

We all need a place to live. Some people live alone, while other people live with their friends or family. Both choices have good and bad points, but which way of living is better?

Thinking about the events in the table below, decide if it is better to live alone or with other people. Explain your reasons.

Event	Live Alone or Live with Other People	Reason
Watching a Movie		
Feeling Sick		
Christmas Day		
Feeling Hungry		

Warm-Up Questions

1. Have you ever been alone in your home? Did you like it?

2. What are some good things about living with your family?

3. Do you want to live alone when you are older?

Live Alone or With Other People?

When you come home, do you like to be the only person there? Or do you enjoy having other people around you? We can choose to live alone or share a home with other people. Which choice do you prefer?

Some people say that having a home that you do not share is an excellent way to live. A great benefit of living alone is that your home will be quiet. After studying or working hard all day, people just want to relax. They don't want other individuals to bother them. This is possible if a person lives alone. Another advantage is that you can do anything that you want in your home. You can listen to music, watch TV, or take a nap because no one will interrupt you.

Other people say that sharing a home with other people is better than living alone. People who live in the same home will not be lonely because there will always be someone to talk to or play with. This helps people not to become lonely or depressed. In addition, people who live together have fewer chores to do. This is because everybody can do some housework. As a result, people who share a home will have more free time.

Comprehension Check

Answer the questions using information from the reading passage.

1. What choice do we need to make about living in a home?

2. What do people want to do after studying or working hard all day?

3. Why is it easy to watch TV or take a nap if you live alone?

4. Why will we not be lonely if we live with other people?

5. Why do people who live together have more free time?

Vocabulary Check

Complete each sentence with one of the words below.

bothers	share	interrupt	depressed	nap

1. We shouldn't _____ teachers if they are talking to other people.

2. My father likes to take a _____ after eating lunch.

3. I felt _____ after getting low scores on my school tests.

4. My little brother always _____ me when I am trying to do my homework.

5. My friends and I _____ our snacks during break time.

Opinion Practice

Practice supporting and refuting the opinions below.

 Supporting Opinions

1. Living with other people is safer and easier…

2. Living alone is less stressful…

3. It is cheaper for people to live together…

4. If you live alone, you can be either tidy or messy…

ⓐ because there will be no arguments.
ⓑ because there is always somebody who can help you.
ⓒ because they can share the rent and bills.
ⓓ because you don't need to worry about other people.

 Refuting Opinions

1. There are fewer chores to do if you share a home with other people.

2. People who live together will not be lonely.

3. It is great to relax alone in a quiet home.

4. People who live alone can organize their homes just the way they like them.

ⓐ I'm not sure about that. Most individuals like to talk to other people about their day or problems they have.
ⓑ That depends. Some people are very lazy and don't do any housework at all.
ⓒ I'm not sure about that. People who live alone need to think about organizing their homes better when their friends visit their places.
ⓓ That depends. Some people who live together don't see each other much because they are busy.

Opinion Examples

Read the opinions and answer the questions.

 Supporting Opinion

It is much better to live alone. The first reason is that it is less stressful. People who live on their own will never have an argument. They can eat what they want. They can also come home when they want to. Nobody gets angry with them. The second reason is that people living alone can control how they organize their homes. They can choose the furniture, the colors, and even the type of home. As a result, people who live alone will have a home that is perfect for them.

 Opposing Opinion

Sharing a home with other people is a much better way to live. To begin with, it is much cheaper to share a house or apartment. This is because we can share the costs of rent, gas, and water with other people. As a result, people who share will have more money to save. They will also have more money to spend on things that they need. In addition, there will always be somebody who can help. Sometimes we need help if we get hurt or need to fix something. It is good to know that we will not be alone.

1. Circle the main idea in each opinion.

2. Underline the supporting ideas in each opinion.

3. Can you think of some examples to support the ideas in each opinion?

Discussion Questions

Discuss these questions in groups.

1. Do you like a home with some noise? Why?

2. When you go home, do you like to be alone or be with other people?

3. Do you think people who live together should share the chores?

4. Is it important to live in a home that you have decorated?

5. Do you think people who live together argue a lot?

Let's Debate

Choose one of the statements below and then debate in groups.

1. It is better to live alone than to live with other people.

2. Living with your family is better than living with your friends.

3. People who share a home don't feel depressed.

Unit 12
School Field Trips Are Great

Every year, schools all around the world take their students on trips to different places. These trips are usually fun for the students. But are they a good way to spend time and money?

Imagine that your teacher asks you to plan a field trip for your class. Think about where you will go and for how long. Then, think of the activities your class will do. Remember to write down the things your class will learn on this trip.

Field Trip Location	
Field Trip Length	
Class Activities	
Things the Class Will Learn	

Warm-Up Questions

1. Have you been on a school field trip? Where did you go and what did you do?

2. Do you think field trips are enjoyable?

3. Should students decide where to go for the school field trip?

School Field Trips Are Great

Teachers take their students on a field trip every semester. This is a tradition that has happened for a long time. However, many parents and teachers doubt if class trips are a good idea.

Some people say that there are good reasons to continue going on school field trips. One reason is that they are a great experience. Students get to leave school for a day or even longer. And they visit a new place they may see in a book. Another reason is that students and teachers can spend more time together. This is good because they can talk and learn more about each other. A class where students are good friends is a great place to learn.

Other people say that there are many problems with field trips. One reason is that students don't usually learn much. This is because they often go to amusement parks or movie theaters. This is a waste of a school day. Instead, students can learn subjects like math or science.

Another reason is that field trips are usually expensive. Schools sometimes fund the trip, but parents usually have to pay. These days, parents don't have a lot of extra money to pay for a trip that is not important.

Comprehension Check

Answer the questions using information from the reading passage.

1. How often do teachers take their students on field trips?

2. Why are field trips a great experience?

3. Why is it good for teachers and students to spend more time together on field trips?

4. Students often don't learn much on field trips. Why?

5. Why is it a problem if field trips are expensive?

Vocabulary Check

Complete each sentence with one of the words below.

fund	expensive	semester	tradition	experience

1. It is a(n) _____ in my family to go for a walk together every weekend.

2. I have stopped buying comic books because they are too _____.

3. My family and friends helped to _____ my trip to Australia.

4. Each school _____ is about four months long.

5. It was a great _____ to visit Italy. I learned so much about its history, culture, and food.

Opinion Practice

Practice supporting and refuting the opinions below.

 Supporting Opinions

1. Students learn and remember many things on a field trip…

2. Field trips should be fun…

3. Field trips are not a good use of teachers' and students' time…

4. Field trips are dangerous…

ⓐ because many students get lost and hurt every year.

ⓑ because they can see, touch, and experiment with things in real life.

ⓒ because teachers need to spend a lot of time planning the trip and students sit on a bus for a long time doing nothing.

ⓓ because they are special events that children remember for a long time.

 Refuting Opinions

1. Field trips are important because teachers and students can spend time together.

2. Field trips to amusement parks and other fun places are a silly idea.

3. Field trips are too expensive.

4. Field trips help students learn more about the world.

ⓐ No, they're not. Fun trips can be a great experience for students. Also, these trips can be a reward for working very hard all semester.

ⓑ I disagree. Students don't learn anything new about the world because they have been to the same places many times before.

ⓒ We don't need field trips to spend time together. We can talk to each other at break time, at lunchtime, and after school.

ⓓ This doesn't need to be true. Field trips can be cheap or even free. Many museums sell very cheap tickets to schools.

Opinion Examples

Read the opinions and answer the questions.

 Supporting Opinion

 **35** / Unit 12

Schools must continue taking students on field trips. The first reason is that students can learn and remember so many things from a field trip. They can learn not only about subjects such as science and art, but also about our society. The second reason is that field trips are a great way to get students to study hard during the semester. This is because teachers will reward their class with a great trip. Therefore, the students will study hard and also have a little bit of fun, too.

 Opposing Opinion

 **36** / Unit 12

Field trips are an old idea and we need to stop them. One important reason is that these trips are a waste of time. Teachers need to spend many hours organizing the trip instead of planning their lessons. And students need to have a few days away from school. Another reason is that field trips are dangerous. Many accidents can happen when teachers and students travel to new places. Large groups of children should stay in their school because it is much safer.

1. Circle the main idea in each opinion.

2. Underline the supporting ideas in each opinion.

3. Can you think of some examples to support the ideas in each opinion?

Discussion Questions

Discuss these questions in groups.

1. Do you think students learn many things on field trips?

2. What do you think is the most important reason for a field trip?

3. Do you think field trips are dangerous?

4. Do you think a cheap field trip can still be fun?

5. Will the chance to go on a good field trip help you to study hard during the semester?

Let's Debate

Choose one of the statements below and then debate in groups.

1. Schools should not have field trips.

2. Schools should only have field trips to museums.

3. A field trip should only last for a few hours.

Unit 13
More Tourists in South Korea

The number of people visiting South Korea is increasing every year. The government wants even more people from foreign countries to come. Is more tourism good for Korea?

Imagine that you have to plan a three-day trip for people visiting South Korea. What places should they see and why? Tell your classmates about your ideas.

Day	Places to Visit in South Korea	Why It Is Important to Visit These Places
Day 1		
Day 2		
Day 3		

Warm-Up Questions

1. Do you think South Korea is a good place for a vacation?

2. Which city is the best place that you have visited in South Korea?

3. What things may be difficult in Korea for a foreign tourist?

More Tourists in South Korea

Over ten million people visit South Korea every year, and this number is growing. All these tourists visiting the country may sound wonderful. But will it cause problems?

Some people say that drawing more tourists to Korea is a great thing. When people go on vacation, they spend a lot of money. Tourists spend money on hotels, food, and sightseeing. All this money helps to make Korea richer. Another benefit of more tourists is that Koreans will construct many great things. They will build new hotels, resorts, roads, and train networks for tourists and Korean residents to use. As a result, visitors will have a great time. At the same time, Korean residents will have a higher quality of life.

Other people say that drawing more people to Korea causes problems. One reason is that everything becomes more expensive. The price of transportation, restaurants, and hotels will increase because many people want to use them. This is a big problem for people who live in Korea because they will have less money. Another problem is that tourists may pollute the environment. They may ruin beautiful beaches and national parks.

Comprehension Check

Answer the questions using information from the reading passage.

1. How many people visit South Korea each year?

2. Why do tourists spend a lot of money when they are on vacation?

3. Why can more tourism help Korean residents to have a higher quality of life?

4. Why will people who live in Korea have less money if there are too many tourists?

5. What will happen to the environment if there are too many visitors?

Vocabulary Check

Complete each sentence with one of the words below.

constructed	residents	ruined	sightseeing	transportation

1. The _____ who live in my apartment building have a meeting once a month.

2. I really like to go _____ when I visit new places.

3. My white shirt is _____ because I washed it with a red sock.

4. Korea's _____ is great. It is easy and cheap to travel around the country.

5. My sister is really happy because they _____ a new department store close to our home.

Opinion Practice

Practice supporting and refuting the opinions below.

 Supporting Opinions

1. There will be more jobs for people in Korea if there is more tourism…

2. More tourists will make Korea more famous…

3. Many tourists can make local residents angry…

4. A lot of visitors can cause more pollution…

ⓐ because their towns and cities will change too much.

ⓑ because people will need to build things and work in hotels and other places.

ⓒ because tourists often ruin beautiful beaches and national parks.

ⓓ because the visitors will learn about Korean culture and tell their friends.

 Refuting Opinions

1. Things will become too expensive if there are too many tourists.

2. Tourists will ruin natural areas.

3. People will learn more about Korean culture.

4. If more tourists visit Korea, there will be more jobs.

ⓐ Actually, things may become cheaper because businesses want visitors to eat, go shopping, or stay with them.

ⓑ I doubt it. Most people on vacation in Korea will just go shopping, eat, and have fun. They do not care about Korean culture.

ⓒ This may be true. However, many jobs will be low-paid and part-time.

ⓓ This is not true. More visitors can help protect the environment because the government will have more money to keep the areas clean.

Opinion Examples

Read the opinions and answer the questions.

 Supporting Opinion

More tourists visiting South Korea will be really great for the country. A big benefit of more visitors is that there will be more jobs for people who live in Korea. This is great because the workers will spend their money in Korea. And this will help to create more jobs. In addition, Korea will become more famous. Visitors will learn more about Korea, its history, food, and culture. When these people go home, they will tell their friends and family about the things they have learned in South Korea.

 Opposing Opinion

More people visiting Korea will cause many problems. One problem is that local people will become angry with tourists. This is because their towns and cities will change too much. People will build many things so that tourists visit and spend money. Another problem is that many things such as housing, food, and transportation will become more expensive. This is a big problem for Korean residents. They may even need to move because living in an area popular with tourists is just too expensive.

1. Circle the main idea in each opinion.

2. Underline the supporting ideas in each opinion.

3. Can you think of some examples to support the ideas in each opinion?

Discussion Questions

Discuss these questions in groups.

1. Is it a good thing that more people will see Korea's beautiful national parks and beaches?

2. What things should Korea build so that more tourists come to Korea?

3. Do you prefer cheap but slow transportation or fast but more expensive transportation? Why?

4. Do you think it is important for visitors to learn about Korea?

5. How will you feel if your city becomes bigger and busier because of tourists?

Let's Debate

Choose one of the statements below and then debate in groups.

1. Korea will benefit from more tourists.

2. More tourists visiting Korea will help the country become more famous.

3. Korea needs to build more things so that tourists will come to the country.

Reading Newspapers and Watching the News

Adults usually read or watch the news to find out what is going on in the world. Children usually ignore the news. Is this OK? Or should they study the news at school?

Look at the table below and think of any big events that have happened recently. Tell your classmates about each event.

Event	Name of Event	Details About the Event
Big News Story		
Sports		
Weather		
Technology		

Warm-Up Questions

1. What is the best way to follow the news? Why?

2. How often do you read or watch the news?

3. Do you like to know what things are happening in the world?

Reading Newspapers and Watching the News

Our world is a busy place and many important things are happening all the time. Many students say that they don't have time to read or watch the news. Maybe we should introduce a class about the news in schools.

Some people say that the introduction of a news class in school is necessary. Students are adolescents, but they need to know what is happening in the world. Many events can change the lives of students. Therefore, it is important that they have a chance to read, learn, and discuss what is happening. Another advantage is that students can learn many skills in this class. They will improve their reading, listening, vocabulary, and thinking skills. These are the skills that employers want.

Other people say that a class about the news is unnecessary in school. One reason is that the news changes so much. As a result, the news events that students studied a week ago will become useless quickly. This is a waste of students' time. Another problem is that the news stories may be scary for young people. News about war can worry children and teenagers. Students have many things to do, and they don't need any more stress.

Comprehension Check

Answer the questions using information from the reading passage.

1. Why do many students not read or watch the news?

2. Why should students know what is happening in the world?

3. What are some skills that students can improve by studying the news?

4. Why is it a problem that news events change so often?

5. Studying news articles about war may be a problem for students. Why?

Vocabulary Check

Complete each sentence with one of the words below.

adolescent	introduction	necessary	scary	useless

1. It was _____ when I was stuck in an elevator.

2. A(n) _____ is usually between 12 and 18 years old.

3. These days, it is _____ to learn how to use a computer.

4. The car broke down, so it was _____ .

5. The _____ of the Internet to the world was an amazing event.

Opinion Practice

Practice supporting and refuting the opinions below.

 Supporting Opinions

1. It is good for students to study the news…

2. Students who study the news have many things to talk about…

3. Children and adolescents shouldn't study the news…

4. The news is too difficult for students to understand…

ⓐ because most stories are about bad things. This makes children sad.

ⓑ because they know about many things happening in the world.

ⓒ because they are too young to understand the world.

ⓓ because they can get good scores in school assignments.

 Refuting Opinions

1. Students can improve their vocabulary by studying the news.

2. It is important for students to know what is happening in the world.

3. The news is too difficult for students to understand.

4. Students shouldn't study news stories because they change so quickly.

ⓐ There are much better ways than studying the news to improve students' vocabulary skills.

ⓑ That doesn't matter. Students learn many important skills by studying the news.

ⓒ Not really. Students need to focus on their studies to get good scores. They don't need to know what is happening in places far away.

ⓓ This is not true. There are many simple news articles and the teacher can explain them, too.

Opinion Examples

Read the opinions and answer the questions.

 Supporting Opinion

 **41** / Unit 14

Students should study the news in school. One reason is that everybody, including young people, needs to know what is happening in the world. Students who watch or read the news can understand our world. Another benefit is that students can learn skills that will help them to be successful. When a teacher discusses the news with his or her class, the students can learn general knowledge. They also learn to think about what is right and what is wrong.

 Opposing Opinion

 **42** / Unit 14

It is not a good idea for students to study the news in school. First, students have so many subjects to learn. Adding one more subject does not help the students. Adolescents need to get good scores in subjects like Korean, math, English, and science. The news is not important. Second, almost all news stories are about bad things. Young people don't need to know about horrible stories. They are young and should be happy.

1. Circle the main idea in each opinion.

2. Underline the supporting ideas in each opinion.

3. Can you think of some examples to support the ideas in each opinion?

Discussion Questions

Discuss these questions in groups.

1. Do you think students have enough time to study the news in their free time?

2. Is it important to know what is happening in other countries?

3. Should we believe everything that we see in the news?

4. Do you think studying the news will be more fun than studying other school subjects?

5. At what age should students begin reading the news?

Let's Debate

Choose one of the statements below and then debate in groups.

1. Students should study the news in school.

2. Students should only read newspaper articles during their news class.

3. Students shouldn't study the news until they are in high school.

Unit 15
Working at Home

Most people have to get up early in the morning to go to work. They need to work all day long. After finishing work, they need to travel home again. Will it be better if we work from home?

Most adults work for eight hours a day. Imagine that you are working at home. Complete the table below. Tell us where you will work, what time you will start and finish work, and what things you will do in your free time. Tell your partner about your day.

Where You Will Work in Your Home:

Start Time: _____ a.m. / p.m.   Finish Time: _____ a.m. / p.m.

Time	Activity	Reason
Break Time (15 minutes)		
Lunchtime / Dinnertime (1 hour)		
Break Time (15 minutes)		

Warm-Up Questions

1. Does working at home sound like a good idea?

2. If you work at home, what clothes will you wear? Why?

3. What is the best room to work in at home? Why?

Working at Home

Going to work five or six days a week is tiring. These days, however, technology has really improved. As a result, we can do all our work at home. More and more people are working from home, but is it a good way to work?

Some people say that working from home is an excellent idea. One reason is that workers don't have to commute to work every day. As a result, people will have more time to work or do other activities. Another benefit is that people who work at home are much happier. They can work in any room that they like. They can eat snacks, and they don't have to sit next to annoying co-workers.

Other people say that working from home has problems. One problem is that people may not be motivated to work if their bosses cannot see what they are doing. At home, there are too many fun things to do such as watching television, playing computer games, or just surfing the Internet. Another problem is that workers who stay at home cannot easily meet other workers to discuss work. This means that workers will not carry out their assignments very well.

Comprehension Check

Answer the questions using information from the reading passage.

1. Why can people work from home these days?

2. Why will people who work from home have more time?

3. Workers who work from home will be happier. Why?

4. Why may people who work at home not be motivated to work?

5. Why will workers who work at home not carry out their assignments very well?

Vocabulary Check

Complete each sentence with one of the words below.

co-worker	motivated	boss	commute	assignment

1. My father's _____ is terrible. He makes all the workers work for many hours.

2. I am _____ to get good scores this year because my parents will buy me a new smartphone.

3. My mother and her _____ at work are best friends.

4. It is not fun to _____ at rush hour because the roads are too busy.

5. I didn't do my school _____ because I forgot about it.

Opinion Practice

Practice supporting and refuting the opinions below.

 Supporting Opinions

1. People who work at home will do more work during the day…

2. If people work at home, our environment will be cleaner…

3. It can be difficult to concentrate when working at home…

4. It is boring to work at home…

ⓐ because they will be less tired.

ⓑ because your family or pets can bother you all the time.

ⓒ because people don't travel to different places.

ⓓ because people will not use their cars to travel to work every day.

 Refuting Opinions

1. People will waste their time if they work at home.

2. It is difficult for workers to contact their co-workers who work at home.

3. People feel much happier working at home.

4. People who work at home will have more free time.

ⓐ Actually, this is not true. People who work at home work longer hours because they worry that they are not doing enough work.

ⓑ People who work in the office waste their time, too. In fact, they probably waste more time.

ⓒ This is not true. Workers can use emails or smartphones to get in touch with each other.

ⓓ Not really. Many people who work at home often feel lonely and miss working with their co-workers at the office.

Opinion Examples

Read the opinions and answer the questions.

 Supporting Opinion

 **44** / Unit 15

More people should work from home. This is because it will help to make our environment cleaner. Most people drive their cars to work. Cars cause a lot of pollution. Therefore, fewer cars on the road will improve our environment. Another advantage is that workers will be less tired. They will be healthier and happier. These workers will do more work each day. As a result, their companies will be more successful. The workers will not get sick or stressed.

 Opposing Opinion

 **45** / Unit 15

It is not a good idea for people to work at home. Workers may enjoy being at home for a short time. But they get bored very quickly. A bored person will not be a good worker. Therefore, it is much better for workers to work in an office together. In the office, many exciting things happen every day. In addition, it is hard to concentrate when working at home. Workers will think about things they need to do such as the laundry. It is much easier to concentrate on work in an office.

1. Circle the main idea in each opinion.

2. Underline the supporting ideas in each opinion.

3. Can you think of some examples to support the ideas in each opinion?

Discussion Questions

Discuss these questions in groups.

1. Do you think it will be difficult to concentrate on your work if you stay at home? Why?

2. Will you be happy to stay at home all day? Why? Why not?

3. Do you like to meet other people face to face? Or do you prefer sending them emails or text messages?

4. Will it be more difficult to work as a team if people are not in the same room?

5. Imagine that you are the boss. Do you want your workers to work in the company office or at home? Why?

Let's Debate

Choose one of the statements below and then debate in groups.

1. More people should work from home.

2. It is difficult to communicate with others when we work at home.

3. It is boring to work at home.

Unit 16
Do Sports Stars Earn Too Much Money?

Sports stars are very popular. These athletes earn much more money than most people. Do you think they are paid too much money?

Which professions should be paid the most money? Rank the following jobs according to who should be paid the most. Explain your reasons to the class.

soldier	doctor	sports player
cleaner	police officer	

	Job	Reasons
1.		
2.		
3.		
4.		
5.		

Warm-Up Questions

1. Do you have a favorite sports star? Why do you like him or her?

2. Do you want to be a sports star? Why?

3. Will people want to be sports stars if they don't earn a lot of money?

Do Sports Stars Earn Too Much Money?

People often think about how much money sports stars earn each year. Many people are shocked when they learn how much sports stars are paid. They think it is too high. Are they correct?

The majority of people think that sports stars' pay is excessive. In other words, most people believe that sports stars earn too much money. One reason is that sports are not important. They are just games. Fans may be upset if their favorite team loses. But nothing bad will happen to anyone. Another reason is that sports stars don't really help to make our society better. Police officers, doctors, and teachers do very important jobs that help everybody. But they are paid much less than athletes.

There are some people who believe that athletes are not paid too much. To begin with, sports stars have exceptional skills. In other words, they have very good skills. They can play sports better than ordinary people. Anybody with amazing skills earns a lot of money. Another important reason is that sport stars have very short careers. They need to earn a lot of money before they retire. Many athletes don't have much education. Therefore, they cannot get good jobs when they finish playing sports.

Comprehension Check

Answer the questions using information from the reading passage.

1. How do many people feel when they learn how much athletes are paid?

2. Why are sports not important?

3. Which people do important jobs in our society?

4. Why can sports stars play sports better than ordinary people?

5. Why do athletes need to earn a lot of money before they retire?

Vocabulary Check

Complete each sentence with one of the words below.

exceptional	excessive	majority	shocked	retire

1. Doing a(n) [   ] amount of exercise is bad for our health.

2. My mother was [   ] when she saw how dirty my bedroom was.

3. Many people like to travel after they [   ] from work.

4. In Korea, the [   ] of people live in cities.

5. The food at my favorite restaurant tastes [   ].

Opinion Practice

Practice supporting and refuting the opinions below.

 Supporting Opinions

1. Sports stars deserve to earn a lot of money…

2. Athletes should be paid less money…

3. It is not fair that sports stars are paid so much…

4. It is a good idea to pay sports stars a lot of money…

ⓐ because they make people happy all over the world.

ⓑ because they don't help to make our society better.

ⓒ because they will play even better and win many games.

ⓓ because they can still live a good life without much money.

 Refuting Opinions

1. Athletes need to be paid a lot of money because their careers are short.

2. All sports stars are paid too much money.

3. Athletes work only a few hours a day. They shouldn't be paid a lot.

4. Athletes who are paid more will play better.

ⓐ I disagree. They will become lazy because they are too rich. They don't have to try hard.

ⓑ This is not true. Only a few athletes make a lot of money. Many athletes don't earn much at all.

ⓒ Maybe athletes should be paid well, but they don't need millions of dollars a year.

ⓓ They work a few hours a day because they need to rest. If they train too much, they will not play well.

Opinion Examples

Read the opinions and answer the questions.

 Supporting Opinion

 **47** / Unit 16

Sports stars are paid too much money. One reason is that anybody can play sports. There are many ordinary people who can play sports very well. These people can play sports for free. Another reason is that sports stars don't work much. They train for a couple of hours a day, and then they go home to relax. It is not fair when other people work many hours each day and don't get paid much.

 Opposing Opinion

 **48** / Unit 16

Athletes should be paid a lot of money. To begin with, sports stars make people happy all over the world. These fans buy tickets and other items from their favorite teams. These teams make a lot of money. As a result, the players should be paid a lot of money for their hard work. In addition, many athletes only earn a lot of money if they are successful. They need to work very hard. They have to beat the best players in the world. They deserve their high pay.

1. Circle the main idea in each opinion.

2. Underline the supporting ideas in each opinion.

3. Can you think of some examples to support the ideas in each opinion?

Discussion Questions

Discuss these questions in groups.

1. Do you want to be a well-paid sports star?

2. Do you think sports stars should work more?

3. Are sports stars important for our society?

4. Do you want to pay to watch sports players with ordinary skills?

5. Do you think money helps athletes to try harder?

Let's Debate

Choose one of the statements below and then debate in groups.

1. Sport stars are paid too much.

2. Sports stars' pay should be cut.

3. We don't need professional sports.